T0149361

DESCENDANTS OF SLAVE OWNERS IN AMERICA

REPENT AND RELEASE!

LEARN YOUR TRUE IDENTITY IN THIS LAND OF PLENTY BLACK MEN AND BLACK WOMEN

DORIS SAULS

DESCENDANTS OF SLAVE OWNERS IN AMERICA
REPENT AND RELEASE!

iUniverse books may be ordered through booksellers or by contacting:

iUniverse
1663 Liberty Drive
Bloomington, IN 47403
www.iuniverse.com
1-800-Authors (1-800-288-4677)

ISBN: 978-1-5320-7932-0 (sc)
ISBN: 978-1-5320-7933-7 (e)

Library of Congress Control Number: 2019910889

Print information available on the last page.

iUniverse rev. date: 07/31/2019

CONTENTS

ACKNOWLEDGMENT

The late, Mrs. Shirley LaBlanche and I walked the streets of Houston, Texas, Third Ward and Sunnyside during the 1980s praying with the Black Brothers sitting under the trees playing dominoes and just fellowshipping with one another. Shirley would always tell me, we are JEWS, but she could not show me in the bible. So, I did not pay much attention to her statements. Through the faith teaching of Pastor Gene A. Moore, Sr., God revealed to me the reason why we (Black Men and Black Women) were in America. Then, later, as God isolated me in Navasota, Texas, my home town; God began to prophesy to me daily and yearly as I was ushered into HIS presence revealing the contents of this book. This book is a labor of love with God from January, 2012 until January, 2018. ALL GLORY TO OUR PRECIOUS FATHER, THE GOD OF THE ANGEL ARMIES AND HIS SON LORD JESUS CHRIST OF NAZARETH!

Pastor Gene A. Moore, Sr. taught us of The Saint Agnes Church, March of Faith Ministries, Houston, Texas, how to be "God Inside Minded" or practice the presence of God. Applying this principle by God's grace, strength, mercy and diligence, this book is manifested for HIS GLORY ALONE.

Also, I want to give special thanks to Evangelist Lynda Porch for her time and attention to proofreading this work.

DEDICATION

MESSAGE TO MY AFRICAN AMERICAN BROTHERS
AND SISTERS: MATTERS NOT WHAT NAME WE ARE
CALLED, THIS IS WHO WE ARE (JUDAH – PRAISE)!
IT IS DEDICATED TO OUR ENLIGHTENMENT
AND BLESSING IN THIS HOUR. IN THE WORDS
OF OUR ELDER BROTHER JESUS BY
MATTHEW 19;30 -BUT MANY THAT ARE FIRST,
SHALL BE LAST; AND THE LAST SHALL BE FIRST.
AUGUST 20, 2019 – 400 YEARS OVER!

ALSO, MY SLAVE GREAT, GREAT GRANDFATHER:
ELI RANDON AND
MY SLAVE GREAT, GREAT GRANDMOTHER:
MATILDA "TILDY" RANDON
who endured the punishment, hardship and pain that I and
my family might live in the LIGHT of OUR LORD
JESUS CHRIST!

DESCENDANTS OF SLAVE OWNERS IN AMERICA
Repent and Release!

By
Doris Sauls

I

INTRODUCTION

Prophecy: January 10, 2012
Jeremiah 30: 2, 3,10b,11 (NIV, ASB)

This is what the **Lord**, the **God of Israel,** says: Write in a book all the words I have spoken to you. The days are coming, declares the **Lord**, when I bring my people Israel and Judah back from captivity and restore them to the land I gave to their forefathers to possess, says the **Lord**." I will surely save you out of a distant place, your descendants from the land of their exile. I am with you and will save you', declares the LORD. Though I completely destroy all the nations among which I scatter you, I will not completely destroy you. I will discipline you but only with justice; I will not let you go entirely unpunished.

Prophecy: December 27, 2017
Amos 3:8 (NIV, ASB)

The lion hath roared---who will not fear? The **Sovereign Lord** has spoken--- who can but prophesy?

Prophecy: December 27, 2017
Amos 3:11 (AKJV)

Therefore thus saith, The Lord God, an adversary there shall be even around about the land and he shall bring down thy strength from thee, and thy palaces shall be spoiled.

Prophecy: January 5,2018
Numbers 26:19-22 (Message)

Er and Onan were sons of Judah who died early on in Canaan. The sons of Judah by clans: Shelah and the Shelanite clan, Perez and the Perezite clan, Zerah and the Zerahite clan. The sons of Perez: Hezron and the Hezronite clan, Hamul and the Hamulite clan. These were the clans of Judah. They numbered 76,500.

Prophesy: January 14, 2013
Zechariah 2:8, 9 (Message)

God-of-the-Angel Armies, the one of Glory, who sent me on my mission, commenting on the godless nations who stripped you and left you homeless said, "Anyone who hits you, hits me, bloodies my nose, blackens my eye. Yes, and at the right time I'll give the signal, and they'll be stripped and thrown out by their own servants. Then you'll know for sure that God-of-the Angel-Armies sent me on this mission.

Prophecy: December 27, 2017
Amos 3:7 (KJV)

Surely, the Lord will do nothing, but HE will revealethl HIS secret unto his servants the prophets.

Prophecy: December 22, 2017
Psalm 109:27 (KJV)

That they may know that this is thy hand; that thou LORD, hast done it.

Prophecy: February 15, 2012
Micah 7:16 (NIV)

Nations will see and be ashamed deprived of all their power. They will put their hands on their mouths and their ears will become deaf.

Prophecy: January 19, 2012
Isaiah 14: 3, 4b-8 (NIV, ASB)

On the day the **Lord** gives you relief from suffering and turmoil and cruel bondage. How the oppressor has come to an end! How his fury has ended! The **Lord** has broken the rod of the wicked, the scepter of the rulers, which in anger struck down peoples with unceasing blows, and in fury subdued nations with relentless aggression. All the lands are at rest and at peace; they break into singing. Even the pine trees and the cedars of Lebanon exult over you and say, Now that you have been laid low, no woodsman comes to cut us down.

Prophecy: December 22, 2017
Job 36:4 (KJV)

For truly my words shall not be false; **He** that is perfect in knowledge is with thee.

II

WHO IS OUR GOD, GLORY OF OUR GOD

Prophecy: January 17, 2012
Isaiah 46:8-10 (NIV, ASB)

Remember this, fix it in mind, take it to heart, you rebels. Remember the former things, those of long ago. I am **God,** and there is no other. I am **God**, and there is none like me. I make known the end from the beginning, from ancient times, what is still to come. **I say: My purpose will stand, and I will do all that I please.**

Prophecy: December 22, 2017
Proverb 15:3 (NIV, ASB)

The eyes of the **Lord** are everywhere, keeping watch on the wicked and the good.

Prophecy: December 22, 2017
Job 34:21 (NIV, ASB)

HIS eyes are on the ways of men, **HE** sees their every step.

Prophecy: December 26, 2017
Job 31:4 (NIV, ASB)

Does not HE see my ways, and count my every steps?

Prophecy: January 7, 2012
Job 34:21-26 (NLT)

For GOD watches how people live; he sees everything they do. No darkness is thick enough to hide the wicked, from HIS eyes. We don't set the time when we will come before God in Judgment. HE brings the mighty to ruin without asking anyone, and HE sets up others in their place. HE knows what they do, and in the night he overturns and destroys them. HE strikes them down because they are wicked, doing it openly for all to see.

Prophecy: December 26, 2017
II Chronicles 16: 9 (KJV)

For the eyes of the Lord run to and fro throughout the whole earth to show himself strong in the behalf of them whose heart is perfect toward HIM. Herein thou hast done foolishly; therefore from henceforth thou shalt have wars.

Prophecy: December 22, 2017
Psalm 111:2 (AKJV)

The works of the Lord are great, sought out of all them that have pleasure therein.

Prophecy: December 26, 2017
Jeremiah 32:19 (KJV)

Great in counsel and mighty in work; for thine eyes are open upon all the ways of the sons of men: to give everyone according to his ways and according to the fruit of his doings

Prophecy: January 7, 2012
Job 37: 7, 10, 11 (NIV, ASB)

So that all men HE has made may know HIS work, HE stops every man from his labor. The breath of GOD produces ice, and the broad waters become frozen. HE loads the clouds with moisture and scatters HIS lightning through them.

Prophecy: December 22, 2017
Psalm 135:7 (KJV)

HE causes the vapours to ascend from the ends of the earth, HE makes lightnings for the rain, HE brings the wind out of HIS treasuries.

Prophecy: January 7, 2012
Job 37:5,6 (NKJV)

GOD thunders marvelously with HIS voice; HE does great things which we cannot comprehend.

Prophecy: January 17, 2012
Psalm 94:8-11 (NIV, ASB)

Take heed, you senseless ones among the people; you fools, when will you become wise? Does **HE** who implanted the ear not hear? Does **HE** who formed the eye not see? Does **HE** who disciplines nations not punish? Does **HE** who teaches man lack knowledge? The **LORD** knows the thoughts of a man; **HE** knows they are futile.

III

WHO IS "MAN OF WOE"

Prophecy: January 9, 2012, Daniel 7:4,12 (KJV): The first was like a lion and had eagle's wings. I beheld till the wings thereof were plucked, and it was lifted up from the earth, and made stand upon the feet as a man, and a man's heart was given to it. As concerning the rest of the beasts, they had their dominion taken away: yet their lives were prolonged for a season and time.

Prophecy: January 14, 2013
Zechariah 11:5,6a (TLB)

    This will illustrate the way my people have been bought and slain by wicked leaders, who go unpunished. 'Thank God, now I am rich!" say those who have betrayed them—their own shepherds have sold them without mercy. And I won't spare them either, says the **Lord** "for I will let them fall into the clutches of their own wicked leaders and they will slay them.

Prophecy: January 14, 2013
Zechariah 1:14-17 (TLB)

    Then the angel said, "Shout out this message from the **Lord Almighty**: "Don't you think I care about what has happened to Judah and Jerusalem? I am jealous as a husband for his captive wife. I am very angry with the heathen nations sitting around at ease, for I was only a little displeased with my people, but the **nations afflicted them far beyond my intentions**".

DESCRIPTION OF THE MAN OF WOE:

Prophecy: January 7, 2012
Job 27:14-21 (NIV, ASB)

What happens to those who forget to acknowledge The True and Living God, whose name is Jesus, the Christ of Nazareth.

1. However, many his children their fate is the sword.
2. His offspring will never have enough to eat.
3. The plague will bury those who survive him and their widows will not weep for them.
4. Though he heaps up silver like dust and clothes like piles of clay, what he lays up the righteous will wear, and the innocent will divide his silver.
5. The house he builds is like a moth's cocoon, like a hut made by a watchman.
6. He lies down wealthy, but will do so no more, when he opens his eyes all is gone.
7. Terrors overtake him like a flood; a tempest snatches him away in the night.
8. The east wind carries him off, and he is gone; it sweeps him out of his place.

Job 20:10,18, 22 (NIV,ASB)

9. His children will make amends to the poor; his own hands must give back his wealth.
10. What he toiled for must be given back uneaten; he will not enjoy the profit from his trading
11. In the midst of his plenty, distress will overtake him; the full force of misery will come upon him.

Prophecy: January 14, 2013
Zechariah 5:3,4 (NKJV)

Then he said to me, "This is the curse that goes out over the face of the whole earth: 'Every thief shall be expelled', according to this side of the

scroll; and, 'Every perjurer shall be expelled', according to that side of it.".
I will send out the curse," says the **Lord of hosts**; "It shall enter the house
of the thief and the house of the one who swears falsely by **My** name. It
shall remain in the midst of his house And consume it, with its timber and
stones".

Prophecy: January 7, 2012
Exodus 9:17 (NIV, ASB)

You still set yourself against my people and will not let them go.

Prophecy: February 8, 2012
Job 31:13-15 (NIV, ASB)

If I have denied justice to my menservants and maid servants when they
had a grievance against me, what will I do when God confronts me? What
will I answer when called to account? Did not HE who made me in the
womb make them? Did not the same one form us both within our mothers.

Prophecy: December 27, 2017
Amos 3:10 (NIV, ASB)

"They do not know how to do right," declares the LORD, "who hoard
plunder and loot in their fortresses."

Prophecy: February 15, 2012
Isaiah 26:10-11 (NIV, ASB)

Though grace is shown to the wicked they do not learn righteousness,
even in a land of uprightness, they go on doing evil and regard not the
majesty of the LORD. O, LORD your hand is lifted high, but they do not
see it. Let them see your zeal for your people and be put to shame. Let the
fire reserved for your enemies consume them.

Prophecy: January 8, 2012
Isaiah 10:6,7,13,14,25-27 (NIV,ASB)

I send him against a godless nation, I dispatch him against a people who
anger me, to seize loot and snatch plunder, and to trample them down like
mud in the streets. But this is not what he intends, this is not what he has in
mind; his purpose is to destroy, to put an end to many nations. For he says:
"By the strength of my hand I have done this, and by my wisdom, because I

have understanding. I removed the boundaries of nations, I plundered their treasures; like a mighty one I subdued their kings. As one reaches into a nest, so my hand reached for the wealth of the nations. As people gather abandoned eggs, so I gathered all the countries; not one flapped a wing or opened its mouth to chirp. Very soon my anger against you will be directed to their destruction. The **LORD ALMIGHTY** will lash them with a whip, as when **HE** struck down Midian at the rock of Oreb; and HE will raise his staff over the waters as HE did in Egypt. In that day their burden will be lifted from your shoulders (January 2, 2018), their yoke from your neck; the yoke will be broken because you have grown so fat.

Prophecy: January 5, 2013
Micah 7:3,4 (NIV,ASB)

Both hands are skilled in doing evil; the ruler demands gifts, the judge accepts bribes, the powerful dictate what they desire—they all conspire together. The best of them is like a briar, the most upright worse than a thorn hedge. The day of your watchman has come. The day God visits you. Now is the time of their confusion.

Prophecy: February 8, 2012
Isaiah 10:1-4 (NIV,ASB)

Woe to those who make unjust laws, to those who issue oppressive decrees, to deprive the poor of their rights and withhold justice from the oppressed of my people, making widows their prey and robbing the fatherless. What will you do on the day of reckoning, when disaster comes from afar? To whom will you run for help? Where will you leave your riches? Nothing will remain but to cringe among the captives or fall among the slain. Yet for all this, his anger is not turned away, his hand is still upraised.

Prophecy: January 17, 2012
Jeremiah 49:12 (NIV,ASB)

This is what the Lord says, "If those who do not deserve to drink the cup must drink it, why should you go unpunished? You will not go unpunished but must drink it.

IV

WHAT DOES GOD WANT THE MAN OF WOE TO DO?

(DESCENDANTS OF SLAVE OWNERS) REPENT AND RELEASE RICHES BELONGING TO THE PEOPLE OF JUDAH IN AMERICA!

Prophecy: December 22, 2017
Proverb 1:7 (NIV, ASB)

The fear of the Lord is the beginning of knowledge, but fools despise wisdom and discipline.

Prophecy: December 27, 2017
Amos 3;6 (NLT)

When the ram's horn blows a warning, shouldn't the people be alarmed? Does disaster come to a city unless the Lord has planned it?

Prophecy: January 11, 2012
Isaiah 8:10,21 (NIV,ASB)

Devise your strategy, but it will be thwarted, propose your plan, but it will not stand, for God is with us. Distressed and hungry they will roam the land, when they are famished, they will be enraged and, looking upward, curse their king and their God.

Prophecy: August 7, 2016
Amos 9:2-4 (NIV, ASB)

Though they dig down, to the depths of the grave, from there my hand will take them. Though they climb up to the heavens, from there I will bring them down. Though they hide themselves on the top of Carmel, there I will hunt them down and seize them. Though they hide from me at the bottom of the sea, there I will command the serpent to bite them. Though they are driven into exile by their enemies, there I will command the sword to slay them. I will fix my eyes upon them for evil and not for good.

Prophecy: August 2, 2016
Malachi 2:17 (NIV,ASB)

You have wearied the Lord with your words. "How have we wearied HIM?" you ask. By saying, "All who do evil are good in the eyes of the Lord, and HE is pleased with them" or "Where is the GOD of justice?"

Prophecy: December 22, 2017
Job 18:11 (NIV,ASB)

Terrors startle him on every side and dog his every step.

Prophecy: December 27, 2017
Amos 3:15 (NIV,ASB)

I will tear down the winter house along with the summer house, the houses adorned with ivory will be destroyed and the mansions will be demolished," declares the Lord.

Prophecy: January 14, 2013
Zechariah 9:12 (TLB)

Come to the place of safety, all you prisoners for there is yet hope! I promise RIGHT NOW, I will repay you two mercies for each of your woes.

Prophecy: December 27, 2017
Amos 3:3 (KJV)

Can two walk together, except they agree?

Prophecy: February 8, 2012
Isaiah 10:12 (NIV)

Sow for yourselves righteousness, reap the fruit of **unfailing love**, and break up your unplowed ground, for it is time to **seek the Lord** until HE comes and showers righteousness on you.

Romans 10:8,9 (NIV)

But what does it say? "The word is near you; it is in your mouth and in your heart, that is, the message concerning faith that we proclaim: if you declare with your mouth," **Jesus is Lord"** and believe in your heart that God raised him from the dead, you will be saved.

"MAN OF WOE', DO THIS:

Prophecy: January 14, 2013
Zechariah 7:9,10 (NLT)

This is what the Lord of Heaven's Armies says: Judge fairly, and show mercy and kindness to one another. Do not oppress widows, orphans, foreigners, and the poor. And do not plot evil against each other.

Prophecy: January 8, 2012
Isaiah 11:2-4 (NIV,ASB)

The Spirit of the Lord will rest on him-the Spirit of wisdom and of understanding, the Spirit of counsel and of power, the Spirit of knowledge and of the fear of the Lord—and he will delight in the fear of the Lord. He will not judge by what he sees with his eyes, or decide by what he hears with his ears, but with righteousness he will judge the needy, with justice he will give decisions for the poor of the earth. He will strike the earth with the rod of his mouth, with the breath of his lips he will slay the wicked.

Prophecy: January 18, 2018
Zechariah 6:8 (NIV,ASB)

Then he called to me, "Look, those going toward the north country have given my Spirit rest in the land of the north.

V

SLAVERY FOR THE DISOBEDIENT SONS OF JUDAH
(BLACK MEN AND WOMEN IN AMERICA)

Prophecy: January 8, 2017
Genesis 15:13,14 (NIV)

Then the LORD said to him. (ABRAM) Know for certain that your descendants will be strangers in a country not their own and they will be enslaved and mistreated four hundred years (**400 years-August 20, 1619 to August 20, 2019**). But I will punish the nation they serve as slaves, and afterward they will come out with great possessions.

Prophecy: January 5, 2013
Micah 7;18 (NIV/ASB)

WHO IS A GOD LIKE YOU, WHO PARDONS SIN AND FORGIVES THE TRANSGRESSIONS OF THE REMNANT OF HIS INHERITANCE? YOU DO NOT STAY ANGRY FOREVER BUT DELIGHT TO SHOW MERCY. HALLELUJAH, HALLELUJAH HALLELUJAH!!!!!!!!

Prophecy: January 14, 2013
Zechariah 4:6,7 (NIV,ASB)

So HE said to me, "This is the word of the LORD to Zerubbabel: Not by might nor by power, but by my SPIRIT, says the LORD ALMIGHTY. What are you, O mighty mountain? Before Zerubbabel you will become level ground. Then HE will bring out the capstone to shouts of "GOD BLESS IT! GOD BLESS IT!"

Prophecy: January 10, 2012
Isaiah 54:9,10 (NIV,ASB)

To ME this is like the days of Noah, when I swore that the waters of Noah would never again cover the earth. SO NOW I have sworn not to be angry with you, never to rebuke you again. Though the mountains be shaken and the hills be removed, yet my unfailing love for you will not be shaken nor my covenant of peace be removed," says the LORD who has compassion on you.

Prophesy: January 17, 2018
Zechariah 2:10 (Message)

SHOUT AND CELEBRATE DAUGHTER OF ZION. I'M ON MY WAY. I'M MOVING INTO YOUR NEIGHBORHOOD! GOD'S DECREE.

Prophecy: January 5, 2013
Micah 7:15,16 (NLT)

"Yes", says the LORD, I will do mighty miracles for you, like those I did when I rescued you from slavery in Egypt." All the nations of the world will stand amazed at what the LORD will do for you. They will be embarrassed at their feeble power. They will cover their mouths in silent awe, deaf to everything around them.

Prophecy: January 17, 20
Zechariah 1:21 (Message)

"I asked, And what are these all about? HE said, "Since the horns scattered Judah so badly that no one had any hope left, these blacksmiths

have arrived to combat the horns. They'll dehorn the godless nations who used their horns to scatter Judah to the four winds."

Prophecy: January 14, 2013
Zechariah 3:7b (Message)

"Orders from **GOD-OF-THE-ANGEL-ARMIES**: "If you live the way I tell you and remain obedient in my service, then you"ll make the decisions around here and oversee my affairs. And all my attendants standing here will be at your service.

VI

WHAT HAPPENED JUDAH?

Prophecy: September 28, 2016
PSALM 106:21, 22, 24-27, 29, 36-42, 44,45 (NIV, ASB)

They forgot the GOD who saved them, who had done great things in Egypt, miracles in the land of Ham and awesome deeds by the Red Sea. Then, they despised the pleasant land; they did not believe **HIS** promise. They grumbled in their tents and did not obey the Lord. So he swore to them with uplifted hand that he would make them fall in the desert, make their descendants fall among the nations and scatter them throughout the lands. They provoked the **LORD** to anger by their wicked deeds… They worshipped their idols which became a snare to them. They sacrificed their sons and their daughters to demons. They shed innocent blood, the blood of their sons and daughters when they sacrificed to the idols of Canaan and the land was desecrated by their blood. They defiled themselves by what they did; by their deeds they prostituted themselves. Therefore, the **LORD** was angry with HIS people and abhorred his inheritance. **HE** handed them over to the nations and their foes ruled over them. Their enemies oppressed them and subjected them to their power.

But **HE** took note of their distress when **HE** heard their cry. For their sake **HE** remembered **HIS** covenant and out of **HIS** great love **HE** relented.

Prophecy: June 29, 2018
Psalm 106:24-27 (Message)

They went on to reject the Blessed Land, didn't believe a word of what **God** promised, They found fault with the life they had and turned a deaf ear to **God's** voice. Exasperated, **God** swore that **HE'D** lay them low in the desert, Scattering their children hither and yon, strewing them all over the earth.

Prophecy: January 19, 2012
Isaiah 45:14a,b,c,d(NIV, ASB)

This is what the LORD says: The products of Egypt and the merchandise of Cush, and those tall Sabeans---they will come over to you and will be yours; They will trudge behind you, coming over to you in chains, they will bow down before you…

Prophecy: January 8, 2017
Jeremiah 15:14 (NIV Study Bible)

I will enslave you to your enemies in a land you do not know for my anger will kindle a fire that will burn against you.

Prophecy: December 26, 2017

Prophecy: January 8, 2017
Deuteronomy 28:68 (NIV)

The LORD will send you back to Egypt on a journey I said you should never make again. There you will offer yourselves for sale to your enemies as male and female slaves, but no one will buy you.

Prophecy: December 26, 2017
Lamentations 1:9 (Message)

She played fast and loose with life, she never considered tomorrow and now she's crushed royally with no one to hold her hand. Look at my pain, O God! And how the enemy cruelly struts.

Prophecy: December 22, 2017
Deuteronomy 28:41 (KJV)

Thou shalt beget sons and daughters, but thou shalt not enjoy them for they shall go into captivity.

Prophecy: December 26,2017
Lamentations 1;18 (Message)

GOD HAS RIGHT ON HIS SIDE, I'M THE ONE WHO DID WRONG. LISTEN EVERBODY! LOOK AT WHAT I AM GOING THROUGH. MY FAIR YOUNG WOMEN, MY FINE YOUNG MEN, ALL HERDED INTO EXILE.

Prophecy: December 26, 2017
Lamentations 2:22 (Message)

You invited, like friends to a party, men to swoop down in attack, so that on the big day of God's wrath, no one would get away. The children I loved and reared—gone, gone, gone.

Prophecy: December 26, 2017
Lamentations 1:5 (Message)

Her enemies have become her master. Her foes are living it up because God has laid her low, punishing her repeated rebellion. Her children prisoners of the enemy trudge into exile.

Prophecy: December 26, 2017
Lamentation 1:12 (Message)

And you passersby look at me? Have you ever seen anything like this? Ever seen pain like my pain, seen what **HE** did to me, what God did to me in **HIS** rage?

Prophecy: December 26, 2017
Lamentations 1:2 (Message)

She cries herself to sleep each night, tears soaking her pillow. No one's left among her lovers to sit and hold her hand. Her friends have all dumped her.

Prophecy: December 26, 2017
Lamentations 1:16 (Message)re

For all this, I weep buckets, weep buckets of tears, and not a soul within miles around cares for my soul. My children are wasted, my enemy got his way.

Prophecy: December 26, 2017
Lamentations 1:3 {Message)

After years of pain and hard labor Judah has gone into exile. She camps out among the nations, never feels at home. Hunted by all, she's stuck between a rock and a hard place.

Prophecy: March 3, 2018
Lamentations 2:9c (NLT)

Her kings and princes have been exiled to distant lands…

Prophecy: January 6, 2013
Micah 1:11a (NLT)

You people in Shaphir, go as captives into exiles---naked and ashamed.

Prophecy: December 26, 2017
Lamentations 1:21 (Message)

Oh, listen to my groans. No one listens, no one cares. When my enemies heard of the trouble you gave me, they cheered. Bring on Judgment Day! Let them get what I got!

Prophecy: December 26, 2017
Lamentations 1:22a (Message)

Take a good look at their evil ways and give it to them!

Prophecy: February 15, 2012
Isaiah 26:12,13,15 (NIV,ASB)

LORD, you established peace for us; all that we have accomplished you have done for us. O LORD our GOD, other lords besides you have ruled over us, but your name alone do we honor. You have enlarged the nation, **O Lord**; you have enlarged the nation. You have gained glory for yourself; you have extended all the borders of the land.

AUGUST 20, 2019!

Prophecy: December 26, 2017
Lamentations 2:18 (Message)

Give out heart-cries to the **MASTER** dear repentant Zion, let the tears roll like a river, day and night and keep at it, no time outs. Keep those tears flowing.

VII

WHAT DOES JUDAH SAY TO GOD?

Prophecy: April 5, 2012
I Thessalonians 1:9 (ESV)

For they themselves report concerning us the kind of reception we had among you, and how you turned to GOD from idols to serve the LIVING and TRUE GOD.

Prophecy: July 11, 2012
Psalm 74:2 (KJV)

Remember thy congregation, which thou has purchased of old; the rod of thine inheritance, which thou hast redeemed; this mount Zion wherein thou hast dwelt.

Prophecy: December 26, 2017
Zechariah 4:10 (KJV)

For who hath despised the day of small things? for they shall rejoice and shall see the plummet in the hand of Zerubbabel with those seven; they are the eyes of the LORD, which run to and fro through the whole earth.

Prophecy: July 11, 2012
I Kings 8:51 (KJV)

For they be thy people and thine inheritance which thou broughtest forth out of Egypt from the midst of the furnace of iron:

Prophecy: July 11, 2012
Deuteronomy 32;9 (KJV)

For the **Lord's** portion is his people; Jacob is the lot of his inheritance.

Prophecy: July 12, 2012
Psalm 94;14 (KJV)

For the **Lord** will not cast off his people, neither will **HE** forsake his inheritance.

Prophecy: July 11, 2012
Psalm 47:4 (KJV)

HE shall choose our inheritance for us, the excellency of Jacob whom **HE** loved. Selah.

Prophecy: July 11, 2012
Psalm 16:5 (KJV)

The **LORD** is the portion of mine inheritance and of my cup; thou maintainest my lot.

Prophecy: July 11, 2012
Deuteronomy 9:29 (KJV)

Yet they are thy people and thine inheritance, which thou broughtest out by thy mighty power and by thy stretched out arm.

Prophecy: July 11, 2012
I Kings 8:51 (KJV)

For they be thy people and thine inheritance which thou broughtest forth out of Egypt from the midst of the furnace of iron.

Prophecy: July 11, 2012
Psalm 28:9 (KJV)

Save thy people and bless thine inheritance: feed them also and lift them up forever.

Prophecy: January 5, 2013
Micah 7:19,20 (NLT)

Once again you will have compassion on us. You will trample our sins under your feet and throw them into the depths of the ocean. You will show us your faithfulness and unfailing love as you promised to our ancestors Abraham and Jacob long ago.

Prophecy: July 11, 2012
Psalms 68:9 (KJV)

Thou, O GOD, didst send a plentiful rain whereby thou didst confirm thine inheritance when it was weary.

VIII

THE LORD GOD OF THE UNIVERSE REPLIES!

Prophecy: January 8, 2012
Isaiah 11:11 (NIV/ASB)

In that day the **LORD** will reach out **HIS** hand a second time to reclaim the remnant that is left of **HIS** people from Assyria, from lower Egypt, from Upper Egypt, from Cush, from Elam, from Babylonia, from Hamath and from the islands of the sea.

Prophecy: January 17, 2012
Jeremiah 50:41, 42a (NIV/ASB)
II Corinthians 10:4b,5a (NIV/ASB)
Ephesians 6:12 (NIV/ASB)

Look! An army is coming from the north; a great nation and many kings are being stirred up from the ends of the earth. They are armed with bows and spears; On the contrary, they have divine power to demolish strongholds, We demolish arguments and every pretension that sets itself up against the knowledge of God,

For our struggle is not against flesh and blood, but against rulers, against authorities, against the powers of this dark world and against the spiritual forces of evil in the heavenly realms

Prophecy: January 14, 2013
Zechariah 3:4b (NIV/ASB)

See, I have taken away your sin, and I will put rich garments on you.

Prophecy: January 14, 2013
Zechariah 3;9e,10 (NIV/ASB)

And I will remove the sin of this land in a single day. In that day each of you will invite his neighbor to sit under his vine and fig tree, declares the **Lord Almighty.**

Prophecy: December 22, 2017
Ecclesiastes 2:26 (KJV)

For **GOD** giveth to a man that is good in his sight wisdom, and knowledge, and joy: but to the sinner **HE** giveth travail, to gather and to heap up, that **HE** may give to him that is good before **GOD**. This also is vanity and vexation of spirit.

Prophecy: July 11, 2012
Psalm 37;18 (KJV)

The LORD knoweth the days of the upright: and their inheritance shall be forever.

Prophecy: July 11, 2012
Psalm 33:12 (NIV)

Blessed is the nation whose **GOD** is the **LORD**, the people **HE** chose for **HIS** inheritance.

Prophecy: July 12, 2012
Proverb 13:22 (KJV)

A good man leaveth an inheritance to his children's children: and the wealth of the sinner is laid up for the just.

Prophecy: July 12, 2012
Psalm 106:5 (KJV)

That I might see the good of thy chosen, that I may rejoice in the gladness of thy nation, that I may glory with thine inheritance.

Prophecy: February 1, 2012
Deuteronomy 26:16-19 (NIV/ASB)

The **LORD** your **GOD** commands you this day to follow these decrees and laws; carefully observe them with all your heart and with all your soul. You have declared this day this day that the **LORD** is your **GOD** and that you will walk in his ways, that you will keep his decrees, commands, and laws, and that you will obey **HIM.** And the **LORD** has declared this day that you are HIS people, his treasured possession as HE promised, and that you keep all **HIS** commands. **HE** has declared that **HE** will set you in praise, fame and honor high above all the nations **HE** has made and that you will be a people holy to the **LORD** as **HE** promised.

Prophecy: December 22, 2017
Deuteronomy 4;6 (KJV)

Keep therefore and do them, for this is your wisdom and your understanding in the sight of the nations, which shall hear all these statutes and say, surely this great nation is a wise and understanding people.

Prophecy: December 22, 2017 (KJV)
Isaiah 44;24-26 (KJV)

Thus saith the LORD, thy redeemer, and HE that formed thee from the womb, I am the LORD that maketh all things; that stretcheth forth the heavens alone; that spreadeth abroad the earth by myself.

That frustrates the tokens of the liars, and maketh diviners mad; that turneth wise men backward, and maketh their knowledge foolish.

That confirmeth the word of **HIS** servant, and performeth the counsel of HIS messengers; that saith to Jerusalem, Thou shalt be inhabited; and to the cities of Judah, Ye shall be built, and I will raise up the decayed places thereof.

IX

FUTURE GLORY

PROPHECY: JANUARY 9, 2012
DANIEL 7:13,14 (KJV)

I saw in the night visions, and, behold, one like the Son of man came with the clouds of heaven, and came to the ANCIENT OF DAYS, and they brought him near before HIM.

And there was given him dominion, and glory, and a kingdom, that all people, nations, and languages, should serve him: and his dominion is an everlasting dominion, which shall not pass away, and his kingdom that which shall not be destroyed.

AMEN AND HALLELUJAH!

Printed in the United States
By Bookmasters